UNLEASH
THE LEADER
WITHIN

Essential Strategies for Authentic Leadership Success

CONTENTS

DEDICATION

To my family, the Hodge6, Tye, Nekira, Tevon, Jessica, and Justin. You are my insp1ration for everything. At the core of me, my heart, is you. I do it all for you.

INTRODUCTION

Authenticity is not a destination but a journey that begins with the courage to be yourself.

LEADERSHIP IS IN ALL OF US. We all have the potential to be leaders, regardless of our title or role. We all possess leadership skills that can emerge in the right circumstances. While work is often seen as the main domain for leadership, we should not neglect our family. That's where many of us develop our leadership abilities. How do some children turn into natural leaders? They didn't get extra training; their surroundings enabled their leadership qualities to manifest early.

HOW DO YOU LEAD? Our environments influence and form the kind of leaders we are. We often copy what we have seen before. Leaders inspire and managers control. People can sense when leaders care for them; how you behave will determine the impact you make. In this book, I will ask you to look deep inside, to that place of honesty, to define your own leadership. What are the main values that guide you? Being true to yourself builds trust from others. When you act for a higher purpose, when you invest in those around you, we create environments that will develop future leaders.

WHY DO I CARE? My introduction is "I help organizations use people strategies to gain a competitive edge. I love helping people find and use their talents to achieve their dreams." That's my pitch. That's my purpose. This book is a guide to help you find or renew the leader in you and shape your surroundings. I want to inspire everyone to lead authentically and create opportunities for growth. Then, people can be their best, contribute, and work together for common goals. When we are at our best, we give the best to others. It's a ripple effect that creates sparks everywhere. I hope this book motivates you to do the same and boost the talent flow around you. We can and should shine together. Let's begin!

CHAPTER 1: WHAT AUTHENTIC LEADERSHIP IS

True leadership stems from the heart, radiating the light of genuineness in every action.

Reflecting on my own journey, I acknowledge the diverse routes I've followed through various sectors and settings. I used to feel ashamed of my modest origins, but over time, I've learned to appreciate these roots as the core of my leadership philosophy. Each industry and environment I've experienced had its distinctive goals and challenges that have shaped my view on leadership.

I started my career in the healthcare and insurance sector, doing data entry, customer service, and quality assurance. Moving to government contracting made me insecure, as I felt less experienced than others in the field. I tried to hide my lack of knowledge and fit in, but I missed a key chance for self-discovery. It sounds strange, but it's true — knowing oneself is the first step to working well in any situation. And when you don't know your own value, you can be easily overshadowed by others who might see—and maybe use—the unique qualities you have.

My definition of authenticity is straightforward: it's about being genuine, trustworthy, honest, and true to oneself. Similarly, I view leadership as the art of influencing others and cultivating meaningful relationships. Thus, *Authentic*

Leadership to me is the dynamic fusion of these qualities—the genuine and transparent actions employed to inspire and connect with followers. When harnessed, Authentic Leadership empowers us to leverage our innate abilities to uplift others and foster a culture where authenticity is not only accepted but celebrated.

Organizational culture is often seen as a rigid framework, especially in mature organizations where the process of assimilation begins right at the recruitment stage. Onboarding becomes more than an introduction; it's a set of experiences meticulously designed to indoctrinate new hires into the acceptable norms and practices of the company. This cultural gatekeeping tends to filter out those who don't conform. It's a double-edged sword that, while maintaining cultural consistency, can also lead to the loss of good people—those whose potential contributions are misaligned or undervalued by the existing cultural paradigm.

Rather than being harmful, authenticity can be the key factor that transforms an organizational culture. Authentic Leadership shows that being oneself is not only possible but also helpful in a corporate setting. Authentic leaders create environments that are full of trust and collaboration, which are essential for achieving high performance and productivity. Their consistent adherence to their values, especially in challenging times, sets the foundation for integrity and transparency. These leaders demonstrate that authenticity is not just a personal quality but also a strategic resource that, when utilized, can bring immense benefits for the organization.

What makes Authentic Leadership so important to pursue? The answer lies in the universal human need for inspiration and support. Working alongside individuals who are honest, genuine, and trustworthy can have a transformative effect. It breeds a culture where employees are not just willing but eager to deliver their best, where taking risks is not frowned upon but encouraged. This paves the way for innovation and efficiency, fostering a win-win situation. Authenticity might initially seem at odds with established culture, but it holds the power to incite fearlessness. When authentic interactions become the norm, they can spearhead changes with profound and enduring impacts.

There's a motto I live by: fakeness has an expiration date. It's a simple truth that I've seen unfold time and time again. No matter how well-crafted a façade may be, it's unsustainable over a long period of time. The authentic self is a quiet voice that, no matter how hard one tries, will finally speak. Mistakes happen and when they do, they alert that inner gut feeling we all have. We may ignore these signs at first, blinded by the surface, but authenticity can't be hidden for long, showing itself in unplanned moments.

Being genuine is very important-it builds trust and shows that we live by our values. I remember a situation that illustrates this belief: executive leadership decided to give my work to another colleague. To my surprise, that colleague came to me, feeling that something was wrong. This act of honesty made me confront the issue with leadership, even though their explanations for their decision were questionable at best. Throughout this experience, I kept a calm and positive attitude, which led to comments like "She's so nice"—

a phrase that might sound flattering but felt strangely inappropriate, as if hiding a hidden agenda. At times like this, staying true to oneself is more than a personal slogan; it functions as a sign, attracting kind and like-minded people and driving away those with more dishonest intentions. The way you behave, the way you interact with others, leaves a lasting impression on their minds.

As I've navigated through various professional landscapes, I've seen the enduring impact of maintaining an authentic presence. Shine as yourself, because your light guides you and draws others who value and relate to authentic interactions and who will recall not just what you do, but how you affect them. This is the effect of authenticity, one that lasts and changes every place it reaches.

As we wrap up our exploration of *What Authentic Leadership Is*, let's revisit the key takeaways:

- Embrace your unique journey and diverse experiences as they shape your leadership philosophy.
- Understand that self-awareness is crucial in effectively navigating different professional environments.
- Authenticity in leadership is about being genuine and transparent, which inspires trust and connection.
- Authentic Leadership can revolutionize organizational culture, fostering trust, collaboration, and high performance.

- Authentic interactions within the workplace can lead to increased innovation, efficiency, and a culture of risk-taking.
- Being genuine is essential as it builds trust and ensures that your actions align with your words.
- How you conduct yourself professionally can attract like-minded individuals and leave a lasting impact.

Consider these reflection questions to deepen your understanding:

- How have your past experiences shaped your leadership style and philosophy?
- How can you promote and embody authenticity in your leadership role?
- Reflect on a time when being genuine in your professional life led to unexpected outcomes. What did you learn?

CHAPTER 2: WHAT AUTHENTIC LEADERSHIP IS NOT

Leadership is an art, not a mask; it thrives on sincerity, not on pretense.

Authentic leadership goes beyond just seeking power.
You don't understand what real leadership is if you only want to have power and command. Real leadership leans to the right, where serving others is the main priority. Authentic leadership is about sacrificing yourself for the improvement of others. An Authentic Leader's success is not only based on achieving concrete results, but also on their skill to encourage their team to perform well—not by force but by influence.

A true leader always has a strong dedication to serving others. The difference between a leader and a manager is clear—a manager supervises tasks, but a leader inspires employees to achieve their best. While managers are focused on the details of work, leaders are committed to the human element. They support, they direct, they enhance.

Having a title does not make you a leader. Having a label before your name does not show your skill to lead; it only shows how people should address you. The real meaning of leadership is not in titles but in the deeds and duties that go with leading—motivating others, being honest, and building trust. Titles, by themselves, can cause fear or admiration, but they do not automatically earn the respect or loyalty of your team. Think about being a VP: your title alone might cause some level of intimidation. But if you use that intimidation to your benefit, you might create a culture of obedience rather than empowerment. Instead, real leaders involve their followers, asking them to be active contributors to the common vision.

The one-size-fits-all approach to leadership does not acknowledge the unique abilities and interests of team members. Think of a sales leader who relies only on financial incentives to motivate, disregarding those who value recognition or career growth. An authentic leader, however, understands what drives each team member and adapts their approach accordingly, resulting in a more involved and effective team.

Authentic leaders know their own weaknesses and accept them, because they know that leadership is a continuous process of learning and getting better. They don't exaggerate their skills or act fake. Their modesty and willingness to grow make them more approachable and create a bond of trust with their teams. This is what makes real leaders different from hollow leaders who just have titles without meaning.

The quality of leadership is one of the main aspects that can influence how well a project goes. At the same organization that I mentioned in Chapter 1, where business development was the ultimate goal, I was involved in a project that lasted more than four years. However, my work was frequently overlooked or dismissed. The senior leaders saw employees as nothing but revenue sources—valuable resources to be used for securing new contracts. There was no discussion about my personal development; the emphasis was always on getting more out of me for the organization's advantage.

Being genuine is crucial for effective project management, especially when facing complicated and unpredictable scenarios. I had a chance to lead a big project, but I felt doomed to fail. The proposal process was awful; the agency and our partner had bad reputations that made me nervous. Even though the new role was a promotion, I got no extra pay for more work. The advice to "take charge and contribute more" didn't suit my introverted personality. I liked to observe the situation, understand our clients' needs, and build real relationships—bulldozing wasn't my style.

Leading a new team can be challenging, frustrating, and exhausting. We hired new staff from the firm that failed to renew the contract. They had background knowledge and stronger relationships with the clients than us. Our partner was the expert, and we got the job based on their promise of original methods. But they kept their knowledge to themselves, sometimes sabotaging our work. Three different groups—without prior acquaintance—faced challenges to coordinate their objectives.

This project was very hard and frustrating for me and my team at first. The client's representative criticized every mistake but ignored their own contribution to the chaos. I was so busy and anxious that I forgot my purse at home one day—I only thought about work. The leaders were not really leaders. They gave orders, but they didn't inspire.

In my state of feeling overwhelmed, I chose to be authentic rather than compliant. I would say what needed to be said, add value, and handle things my way. I cared more about people than profits. This helped me see things clearly. I noticed how people related, what problems they faced, and led with empathy. Being real—not bossy—let me connect sincerely.

As a leader of a diverse and challenging team, I faced many obstacles, but I also learned important lessons about being genuine. By staying faithful to myself and helping others with honesty, I handled the difficulties of a demanding client, a new role, and a broken team. Leadership wasn't about pretending; it was about being real and caring. And in that situation, I found out what real leadership meant.

As we wrap up our exploration of *What Authentic Leadership is Not*, let's revisit the key takeaways:

- Authentic leadership is about serving others and fostering their growth rather than seeking power for its own sake.
- True leaders inspire and motivate through encouragement and empowerment, not through fear or coercion.
- A leader's role transcends their job title and is defined by their actions, integrity, and the ability to engender trust.
- Effective leadership is adaptable, recognizing and leveraging the unique strengths and motivators of each team member.

- Authentic leaders are self-aware, acknowledging their weaknesses and are committed to continuous learning and self-improvement.

Consider these reflection questions to deepen your understanding:

- How do your actions and daily behavior reflect the title and responsibilities of your leadership role?
- Can you identify a recent situation where adapting your leadership style to an individual's needs led to a better outcome?
- In your leadership journey, how do you ensure that your growth is aligned with the growth of the people you lead?

CHAPTER 3: CORE TENET OF AUTHENTIC LEADERSHIP

Authentic leadership is built on the solid basis of knowing oneself and acting with honesty.

Trust, transparency, and authentic leadership are closely connected principles. Authentic leaders are not just genuine and real in their big actions, but also in their small and steady ones. They do not pretend or lie to manipulate or impress; they act with honesty and integrity, which are the foundations of trust between them and their team members.

Authenticity makes a leader trustworthy, because they are stable, dependable, and constant. Transparency, which means sharing information and decisions openly and clearly, makes this trust stronger. It shows the leader's honesty and respect for the team's contribution to the organization's success. For instance, a leader who communicates their reasons and plans clearly and honestly, becomes a model of trust. These leaders guide their teams and foster a culture where everyone feels respected and knowledgeable. The opposite is the leader who hides their actions or is vague, creating doubt and mistrust that can ruin a peaceful workplace.

There is not only a coincidental connection between authentic leadership, trust, and organizational commitment; it is supported by scientific evidence. A study in The

Leadership Quarterly shows a strong positive link among these factors. When leaders are seen as authentic, employees say they have higher levels of trust and a stronger commitment to their organization. This study supports the claim that trust and transparency are not just optional in leadership; they are necessary for the development of a loyal and productive workforce.

Integrity and ethics are crucial for leadership. They direct the culture of an organization, influencing decisions and behaviors at all levels. Integrity in leadership—shown by honesty, fairness, and consistency—is the foundation of trust in any team or organizational structure. Leaders who have these traits create a safe space for employees—a place where they feel secure, respected, and valued. This space leads to more engagement, productivity, and loyalty. A leader who practices ethical behaviors like openness, transparency, and accountability inspires their team to follow these values. Genuine leaders help their team deal with ethical issues and make decisions that match the organization's core values.

Integrity and ethics in leadership have a significant impact not only within the organization, but also on the public perception and trust that an organization has. In this digital era, where information spreads quickly, a single case of corporate misconduct can turn into a major crisis. A consistent dedication to ethical behavior is a safeguard that preserves an organization's market reputation and, consequently, its financial well-being. Businesses known for their ethical practices often benefit from increased customer loyalty and are more likely to appeal to responsible investors.

Active listening means leaders do more than hear words; they grasp motives, sense hidden feelings, and relate to the core messages that their team members share. This makes trust grow, as employees feel respected and heard. Such a supportive environment is key for innovation, as people can show their creativity without worry of being rejected.

For a true leader, communication is not just telling others what to do. It is a two-way exchange, a continuous discussion that makes the organization's goals and values alive. Good communication is clear, consistent, and ethical, like the leader who models it. It's about being open and truthful, which appeals to both the team members and the outside world, strengthening the organization's reputation and position in the bigger market.

As a leader, I intentionally inspire trust and transparency within my team. Having experienced the challenges of being a team member myself, I strive to ensure that those who work for me don't feel excluded or unheard. But my journey wasn't without its lessons.

I once had a close relationship with a leader—a person I immediately admired and thought I could follow. I was impressed by their style and their skill in inspiring others. It felt very different from an organization where I, as an introvert, often felt excluded. However, when I worked closely with this leader, I started to idealize them—the hero role. I ignored warning signs that showed up later, especially when our relationship moved to a different setting. They became less open, and they gave me information in bits rather than telling me everything. This leader claimed to promote a positive culture, but their actions caused toxicity. They hid a soft tyranny under diplomacy, and they did not do what they said.

This experience taught me an important lesson: I cannot turn a blind eye to unethical behavior, even when it comes from someone I thought I knew or who has a position. As we saw in Chapter 2, real leadership is not about using authority from titles; it's about building an environment that inspires people to excel. I make sure that my actions match my words, promoting honesty and openness.

The foundations of honesty and a healthy culture are vital. As a leader, my aim is to enable those I lead to exceed me. By following these basic principles, I foster a setting where confidence flourishes, openness dominates, and genuineness rules.

Authentic leaders need to be aware of their values, beliefs, and actions, and how they affect their teams. They should ask for feedback and pursue ongoing improvement. By doing these things, authentic leaders motivate and enable their teams, creating a culture that is based on trust and integrity.

As we wrap up our exploration of *Core Tenets for Authentic Leadership*, let's revisit the key takeaways:

- **Trust and Authenticity:** The foundation of authentic leadership is built on trust, which is established through the leader's consistent, genuine actions and behaviors.

- **Transparency in Leadership:** Transparent communication and decision-making processes are critical to fostering trust within a team.
- **Integrity and Ethics:** The consistent demonstration of integrity and ethical behavior by leaders strengthens the trust and commitment of their team members.
- **Cultivating a Positive Culture:** Leaders who operate with honesty and integrity create a positive work culture that encourages engagement, productivity, and loyalty.
- **Active Listening and Communication:** Authentic leaders actively listen and engage in meaningful dialogue, promoting innovation and reinforcing the organization's values.

Consider these reflection questions to deepen your understanding:

- How can you, as a leader, ensure that your actions consistently reflect authenticity and integrity?
- In what ways can you improve transparency within your team or organization?
- How do you actively listen to your team members, and how does this practice influence your leadership style?

CHAPTER 4: DISPELLING IMPOSTOR SYNDROME

The only impostor is doubt, and every leader's truth is their unique strength.

Imposter syndrome is feeling like a fraud despite your achievements and compliments. It's the constant fear that you're pretending to be successful and will be exposed soon. It's a harmful self-doubt that can make you question yourself, feel stressed, anxious, and burned out. You need to identify and overcome this sneaky self-doubt; otherwise, you can't lead others confidently.

In Chapter 1 I introduced my motto, fakeness has an expiration date. It's a simple truth: authenticity is timeless, while pretense is fleeting. Whatever doesn't align with your core will eventually crumble. So how does this relate to Imposter Syndrome? Interestingly, it's almost the opposite. Imposter Syndrome troubles the truly gifted who, despite their significant impact, fail to acknowledge their own talent. It's very different from those who put on a show of competence— a weak appearance of confidence that somehow convinces the world of their skills.

Many skilled people don't realize how good they are, while many fakers act effortlessly. This shows a vital lesson for real leadership: you need to be aware of yourself and your natural talents. Do you know what makes you special? It's not just good to find out; it's necessary. It's how you can reach your potential and lead with true confidence and influence.

When you succeed in the professional world, some people may react with negativity. They may feel threatened or envious of your positive qualities and potential. They may try to belittle your achievements and stop your progress. You need to be strong and overcome these challenges. Keep working on your goals and talents with perseverance. Your talent is yours to grow; don't let it be affected by others. Be proud of your abilities and let your success inspire others. Remember, your journey to reaching your full potential shows your dedication to excellence, not only for yourself, but as a model for those who might look up to you.

To overcome Imposter Syndrome, you need to acknowledge your strengths and weaknesses. It's a process of finding yourself, with the help of others and practical steps. If you want to beat this problem and increase your confidence, here are some things you can do:

- **Keep a journal of your achievements and accomplishments.** Write down the positive feedback you receive, the goals you reach, and the skills you learn. Review your journal regularly to remind yourself of your value and abilities.
- **Seek out constructive criticism and use it as an opportunity to grow.** Instead of fearing failure or rejection, embrace them as part of the learning process. Ask for specific and actionable feedback from people you trust and respect, and implement their suggestions to improve your performance.

- **Practice gratitude and appreciation.** Acknowledge the people who have helped you along the way and express your gratitude for their support. Appreciate what you have achieved and celebrate your progress.
- **Surround yourself with positive and supportive people.** Avoid comparing yourself to others who seem more confident or successful than you. Instead, find mentors, role models, and peers who inspire you and encourage you to pursue your goals. Join a community of like-minded individuals who share your values and vision, and seek their advice and guidance when you encounter challenges or doubts.

These are some of the strategies that can help you overcome Imposter Syndrome and build your confidence as a leader. They are not easy or quick fixes, but rather long-term habits that require consistent practice and commitment. By applying these techniques, you can gradually change your mindset and behavior, and develop a more realistic and positive view of yourself and your capabilities.

As I embarked on the new opportunity detailed in Chapter 2, I found myself in unfamiliar territory. The leader I introduced in Chapter 3 was domineering, and despite frequent discussions about opportunities, they were scarce. It seemed like I was put into a situation that was meant to make me fail.

In my previous project, I had a voice, but it was often stifled if the leader disagreed with my views or if my suggestions didn't align with their agenda. This new opportunity was complicated by the presence of three distinct groups, each with their own objectives. I was subjected to relentless criticism, held accountable for actions I would not have taken, and forced to shoulder the blame for others' mistakes. During this period, I shed many tears. I was in a constant state of anxiety, fearing that I was one phone call away from unemployment.

Eventually, I grew weary of trying to satisfy everyone and decided to let go. I stopped fretting about potential mistakes and focused on my strengths. I began to remember who I was. The work was new, but I already possessed the skills needed to succeed. Once I connected with these skills, I was able to see the situation for what it truly was. I could identify the problems, understand the challenges, and strategize on how to unite the team and deliver exceptional results to our client.

As I leaned into my skills, my senses sharpened. I was able to anticipate outcomes and devise preventative solutions. I was fortunate to have colleagues and family members who understood my situation and offered their support and encouragement. Overcoming Imposter Syndrome is a lifelong journey, but when you put in the work and surround yourself with a supportive community, there's no limit to what you can achieve.

As we wrap up our exploration of **Dispelling Imposter Syndrome**, let's revisit the key takeaways:

- Imposter Syndrome is the internal voice that undermines your achievements.
- Authentic leadership thrives on self-awareness and the recognition of your unique strengths.

- External negativity should not deter you from your path to success.

Consider these reflection questions to deepen your understanding:

- When have you felt like an imposter, and how did you cope with that feeling?
- What are the strengths that define your leadership style?

CHAPTER 5: ENCOURAGING OTHERS AUTHENTICALLY

Authentic encouragement is the kindling that ignites the potential in others.

I think there are times when we could all use a little bit of encouragement. It's not just the presence of encouragement that matters, but its quality and sincerity. Genuine kudos have weight; they resonate with us because they come from a place of authenticity. Moreover, the act of giving commendation must be reserved for those who truly deserve it. Have you ever noticed or been in a situation where a leader provides kudos to people the entire team knows their contributions and efforts are minimal? The leader knows it too, but for whatever reason, they decide that recognition is deserved. The fastest way to lose credibility as a leader is to act inauthentically. As leaders, it is our responsibility to ensure that our words match our actions. Encouragement becomes hollow if it is given to those who do not merit it, running the risk of demotivating those who genuinely contribute and excel. It's about fairness and integrity as much as it is about motivation.

As leaders, we set the tone and create an environment that supports the entire team fairly. This means tailoring your encouragement to align with individual team members' motivations and goals. It's about recognizing the unique drivers of each person and acknowledging their efforts in a way that resonates with them. Understanding when public praise is appropriate and motivating is just as crucial. Some achievements are best celebrated in the spotlight, offering a moment of shared success and recognition. On the other hand, the impact of recognizing contributions in a more intimate and confidential setting is very significant. It conveys a deep level of understanding and appreciation for the individual's effort. This balance of public and private recognition is a testament to a leader's ability to gauge what will best uplift each team member.

While major achievements are cause for celebration, authentic leaders understand the importance of recognizing smaller milestones and wins. This involves acknowledging the incremental successes that contribute to the larger goals of the team. By celebrating both major and minor achievements, leaders create a positive and motivating environment. This form of encouragement reinforces the idea that every effort, regardless of scale, is valuable and contributes to the overall success of the team. It fosters a culture of appreciation where team members feel acknowledged and motivated to continue making meaningful contributions.

Modeling ethical behavior and encouraging others to uphold high ethical standards is fundamental. Authentic leaders, who are honest and clear in their style, have a significant impact on how their team works together. They build an environment of trust within their team with their authenticity. This trust allows for better communication, cooperation, and joint decision-making. Team members are confident in sharing their opinions and suggestions, trusting that they will be listened to and valued. This relationship based on trust inspires employees, strengthens team unity, and boosts overall team performance.

I have a colleague I've worked with for over a decade.
This colleague and I began our work relationship working with
a client that operated in a toxic environment. The environment
was oppressive and made it hard to complete simple
assignments. I remember when having to go to the worksite, I
experienced migraines. We spent time in conference rooms
or bathrooms crying because it was that bad. This colleague
and I were forced into a situation where we were pressured to
deliver, with minimal direction or support. We picked it up,
completed the work, and even received a tiger team award.
The challenging environment allowed us to see the strengths
in each other, rely on each other, and work in a way where
our best was always produced. We didn't have leadership
encouragement or support, but we found it in each other.

**Moving on, an opportunity presented itself where we
could work together again.** Due to us being in the trenches I
knew this colleague was going to be a great addition to the
team. What's interesting is that when we spoke about the
opportunity, the colleague stated, "I don't know how to do this
work". I encouraged my colleague and assured them that they
already possess the skills required for the role. They can
apply many of the skills to different situations; they just need
to adjust them accordingly. Fast forward, this colleague did
the work. The colleague learned what was needed to execute
the job with excellence. What stood out was that the
colleague asked a lot of good questions to help with
comprehension and raised questions if things didn't make
sense. The colleague received a lot of support from many
people and could act in a way that enabled them to act

authentically. I don't think the colleague realized this, but their authentic actions encouraged others on the team.

The colleague's approach to learning, being a student, and figuring out what works for them, set them up as a star performer on the team. This colleague has bloomed because they were authentic at their core. Now that they are in a leadership role, this colleague acts as an authentic leader and keeps using their skills to support the team in a different way. This colleague is praised and recognized for their contributions to the team's success. It all happened because the colleague leveraged their strengths, received authentic encouragement, and learned to move in a way that allowed them to contribute to the team in an authentic manner. This colleague pays it forward by building an environment that encourages others.

By blending these elements of true leadership, we create a support system that improves morale and strengthens the basis of our teams. It's a leadership approach that celebrates the individual while simultaneously elevating the collective, making the whole organization more robust, resilient, and ready for whatever lies ahead.

As we wrap up our chapter on *Encouraging Others Authentically*, let's revisit the key takeaways:

- Authentic encouragement is essential for it to be meaningful and impactful.
- Aligning encouragement with individual team members' motivations and goals fosters a personalized approach.

- Authentic leaders should model ethical behavior and foster a trust-based team culture.
- Trust within the team encourages open communication, collaboration, and improved team performance.

Consider these reflection questions to deepen your understanding:

- In what ways can I better understand the unique motivations of my team members to tailor my encouragement effectively?
- What systems can I put in place to consistently recognize both significant and minor achievements within my team?
- How can I use my authenticity to enhance open communication and collaboration in my team?

CHAPTER 6: HOW TO BUILD TEAMS LEVERAGING AUTHENTICITY

Building teams with authenticity is like weaving a tapestry with threads of trust and respect.

Leadership plays a crucial role in creating a culture of authenticity within teams. It starts with setting the right tone—a tone that reflects transparency, admitting errors, and welcoming vulnerability. By showing authentic behavior, leaders build an environment where team members not only feel safe but also motivated to reveal their true selves. It is a responsibility to recognize and value the different skills and views of each team member. This is more than enhancing individual confidence; it promotes authenticity, emphasizing that team members are respected for who they are, not just their work.

Self-aware authentic leaders are not only role models, but also agents of change. They admit their flaws and promote a culture of learning and improvement for themselves and others. Their honesty about their learning journey encourages team members to grow as well. This culture of learning leads to better problem-solving skills, innovation, and resilience within the team. Teams led by authentic leaders become more flexible and agile, prepared to face challenges and take opportunities.

Effective leadership depends on trust and transparency among teams. This requires clear and candid communication. Leaders should communicate goals, strategies, and choices clearly and truthfully, creating a culture where open discussion is valued. It is essential to establish a secure space where team members can share views and issues without fear.

Leaders can also foster trust and transparency by being vulnerable. They can show that they are human by admitting when they are unsure, recognizing errors, and sharing weaknesses. This shows that they value honesty and authenticity more than pretending to be perfect. This vulnerability inspires team members to be more candid about their own difficulties and missteps.

Inclusivity is essential for authentic leadership. Leaders who care about inclusivity make their teams feel like they belong. This means not only accepting diversity but also looking for and appreciating diverse views. Authentic leaders make sure every team member is listened to and valued. By supporting inclusivity, leaders help team members be themselves at work, making the team more diverse and vibrant. Inclusive leadership, then, is a strong way of motivating, showing that every voice counts.

Feedback is key for authentic leadership. Leaders should promote open communication and regular feedback among the team. This makes the team more dynamic and growth-oriented. One-on-ones are a way to share feedback. Having frequent one-on-ones with each team member will build trust and openness. This means not only giving feedback but also listening to the team's views and ideas. By making feedback constructive instead of critical, leaders enable people to be themselves and help the team succeed. A strong feedback culture leads to continuous improvement and authentic encouragement.

When you take charge of a team that is already functioning, it can be hard to lead with authenticity. In the scenario I mentioned earlier, we hired employees who worked on the previous contract. We also had a partner who was subcontracting with us. There were three groups that had different motivations and perspectives on the work we had to jointly do. For instance, the former contractors cared deeply about the agency's mission. They knew the clients and were enthusiastic about their work. The partner had a lot of expertise in the area of the work we were contracted to do, but from what I saw, they seemed more concerned about keeping their employees billable than adding value to this contract vehicle. The company I worked for was new to this and depended on both parties to help make this work.

To make things worse, a chargeable coworker I knew from before came on board the project. I knew from before that this colleague liked to take charge and lead everything, often crossing and confusing boundaries. The colleague did produce good work, but their behavior was not professional or acceptable. One of the leaders said they were aware of this colleague's difficulties working with others, but they ignored it because of the colleague's good work. This project was full of various and difficult challenges from every side.

As a leader, I aimed to be attentive. I wanted to understand what drove people and how we could work together effectively. I was authentic and gave feedback with tact. If there were disagreements, and there were, then I stepped up to make a decision that suited everyone. I was open about the risks and the requirements to make this successful for everyone involved. I offered my time for calls to talk about tasks or issues. I often volunteered to assist with work so that we could meet our deadlines as a team. I found it essential to connect with the team in different ways such as in groups, with the leads, and with support. I had regular one-on-ones with the new employees that came from the previous contract so that they would feel valued and could adapt to the company better. I fostered an inclusive environment where everyone could express their opinions, worries, and ideas. This was a great opportunity and if we collaborated, then we could produce and contribute to great work.

Being authentic can enhance team building and performance. Authentic leaders are transparent, vulnerable, and accepting of mistakes, which fosters a safe space for team expression. Clear communication and open dialogue are also vital for building trust within a team.

As we wrap up our chapter on *How to Build Teams Leveraging Authenticity*, let's revisit the key takeaways:

- Authentic leadership sets a tone of transparency, vulnerability, and acceptance of mistakes, creating a safe space for team expression.

- Clear communication and the creation of a safe space for open dialogue are fundamental to building trust within a team.
- Leaders who show their human side by admitting mistakes and weaknesses encourage their team to do the same.
- Prioritizing diversity and inclusivity helps build a team where everyone feels respected and heard.
- Authentic leadership influences the broader organizational culture, leading to higher engagement, retention, and performance.

Consider these reflection questions to deepen your understanding:

- How can I more effectively model transparency and vulnerability to my team?
- In what ways can I recognize and celebrate the unique contributions of individual team members to promote a sense of personal value and authenticity?
- How can I ensure that trust and transparency are not just concepts but practiced realities in my day-to-day leadership?
- What steps can I take to create a more robust feedback culture that encourages open communication and continuous personal and team development?

CHAPTER 7: HOW TO LEAD AUTHENTICALLY WITH TEAMS YOU INHERIT

Leading with authenticity transforms inherited teams into families united by shared values.

Assuming a leadership role is a significant event. It's not just about managing tasks, but also about inspiring people, driving change, and making impactful decisions. Authentic leadership is about being true to oneself, upholding ethical standards, and fostering a genuine connection with the team. It's about creating an environment of trust where every voice matters. This trust is built through open and honest communication, which is the first step in this leadership journey. As an authentic leader, your role is to ensure that everyone in the team feels heard, valued, and motivated to contribute to the team's success. This approach not only enhances team collaboration but also boosts individual performance and job satisfaction.

Listening is more than just hearing what someone says. It's about understanding their perspective, their emotions, and their needs. It's about showing genuine interest and curiosity in their ideas, opinions, and experiences. It's about giving them your full attention and avoiding distractions or interruptions. Listening is a skill that authentic leaders practice and improve constantly, as it is essential for building trust and rapport with the team. As an authentic leader, your role is to ensure that everyone in the team feels heard, valued, and motivated to contribute to the team's success. This approach not only enhances team collaboration but also boosts individual performance and job satisfaction.

Transparency, as a key aspect of authenticity, plays a vital role in leadership. It involves the open and honest sharing of information, decisions, and actions. When leaders are transparent, they create an environment where everyone is privy to the decision-making process. This includes not only the final decisions but also the considerations, discussions, and sometimes even the debates that lead to those decisions. This openness allows team members to see the ups and downs of successes and setbacks. It's not about showcasing only the victories but also about revealing the challenges, the hurdles, and how they are being addressed. This can be a powerful way to demonstrate resilience and perseverance, and it can also provide valuable learning opportunities for the team.

Accountability with compassion helps the team grow. It means setting a high but realistic standard and helping the team meet it. Leaders who are empathic and accountable create a culture where the team shares responsibility and faces challenges together. For example, when a team member fails to deliver on a task, the leader can show compassion by acknowledging the reasons and emotions behind the failure, while also holding them accountable by asking them to reflect on what went wrong and how they can improve. The leader can also offer support and guidance, while also empowering the team member to take ownership of their actions and learn from their mistakes. This way, the leader can foster a growth mindset and a sense of resilience in the team, which can enhance their performance and satisfaction.

The transition period needs patience and strategy. It's a time for the leader to learn about the team and to bring their own methods. It's about getting quick results to improve morale while also working on long-term goals for lasting growth. It's about building relationships until the new and the familiar connect. For example, the leader can conduct a SWOT analysis (strengths, weaknesses, opportunities, threats) of the team and identify the areas that need immediate attention and the areas that have potential for development. The leader can also communicate their vision and values to the team and align them with the organizational goals and culture. The leader can also involve the team in the decision-making process and solicit their feedback and input. The leader can also recognize and reward the team's achievements and celebrate their successes. These strategies can help the leader establish their credibility and authority, while also creating a sense of collaboration and trust within the team.

When I worked at a Federal Agency, I had an opportunity to detail as a supervisor. A detail is when an employee has an opportunity to perform at a higher level for a limited duration such as 90 days. The opportunity was amazing, however it entailed taking over the team I was a part of, what meant I would now be supervising my peers.

Before I became the supervisor, I had to train the team members on our processes and systems. I noticed that one of the team members was struggling and I alerted the previous supervisor, but nothing was done. My new boss knew about the problem and the former supervisor's neglect, and they asked me to solve it. This was a challenging time for me, as I was new to the field. I should also mention that I'm a very introverted person, so dealing with people issues is very difficult for me. As a result, I had a hard time managing my boss's expectations, establishing my authority, and delivering results.

At the time, I was leading a team of two, both of whom were new to the agency. Part of my responsibilities included conducting periodic reviews during their probationary period. This involved providing feedback on their work, highlighting their strengths, and identifying areas for improvement. To ensure success, I established regular check-ins to discuss work-related matters or any other topics they wished to bring up.

Our Agency was conveniently located in Washington, DC, which offered us the opportunity to take walks on the National Mall or visit underground shops and eateries for lunch and conversation. I found that creating the right atmosphere was instrumental in encouraging open communication, learning more about my team members, and fostering an environment conducive to feedback. As an introvert, these strategies were particularly beneficial for me. They helped me feel more comfortable and enabled me to listen attentively, thereby facilitating the development of genuine one-on-one connections with my team members.

One of the challenges I faced as a leader of an inherited team was to balance transparency and transition. I wanted to be clear about my vision, expectations, and goals for the team, but I also wanted to respect the existing work habits and dynamics that had developed over time. I knew that change can be hard and stressful, especially when it comes from a former peer who has not yet established their authority. I discovered in these conversations that most people have a desire to excel and need a chance to show it. They need the appropriate resources and they need direction until they can proceed independently.

As a result, I chose to introduce changes in a gradual and cooperative way. I asked my team members for their views and choices, and I included them in the deciding process as much as possible. I also provided them with regular feedback and recognition for their contributions and achievements. I acknowledged that the transition might not be easy or smooth, but I assured them that I was there to support them and help them grow. The transition took a lot of patience and perseverance, but over time, our authentic interactions allowed us to establish a team dynamic that was positive, productive, and trusting. We learned from each other, challenged each other, and celebrated each other's successes.

Leadership is more than managing tasks; it's about inspiring people, leading changes, and making effective decisions. Authentic leaders are honest with themselves and others, act with ethics, and build real relationships with their teams. They create a trustful environment where everyone's voice matters, by communicating openly and honestly. This helps the team work better together and improve their performance and happiness. Some key skills of this leadership style are active listening, transparent decision-making, compassionate accountability, and strategic patience during changes. These skills help the team develop a growth mindset, resilience, and a sense of teamwork, which ultimately improves performance and happiness.

As we wrap up our chapter on **How to Lead Authentically with Teams You Inherit**, let's revisit the key takeaways:

- Authentic leadership involves being true to oneself, upholding ethical standards, and fostering a genuine connection with the team.
- Trust is built through open and honest communication, and it's crucial for a leader to ensure that everyone in the team feels heard, valued, and motivated.
- Active listening is more than just hearing; it involves understanding perspectives, emotions, and needs, and showing genuine interest in others' ideas.
- Transparency in leadership involves openly sharing information, decisions, and actions, allowing everyone to understand the decision-making process.
- The transition period requires patience and strategy, balancing quick results to boost morale with long-term goals for sustained growth.

Consider these reflection questions to deepen your understanding:

- How can you foster a genuine connection with your team and create an environment of trust?
- What strategies can you use to improve your active listening skills and show genuine interest in your team's ideas?
- How can you increase transparency in your leadership and decision-making processes?
- How can you balance accountability with compassion to foster a growth mindset in your team?
- What strategies can you implement during the transition period to learn about your team, boost morale, and work towards long-term growth?

CHAPTER 8: APPLYING AUTHENTICITY

Authenticity applied is like a signature; it's unique, recognizable, and cannot be replicated.

Taking on a leadership role means more than handling tasks; it means motivating people, leading change, and making decisions that matter. Authentic leadership is defined by self-honesty, ethical integrity, and the development of genuine relationships with team members. It requires the establishment of a trusting environment where every voice is valued, achieved through open and honest communication. This approach enhances team collaboration and boosts individual performance and satisfaction.

Authentic leadership is about using your strengths. You don't have to fit in everywhere but find a place that appreciates and supports what you can offer. Authentic leaders know their skills and make spaces where they can use them well, helping themselves and their teams.

Authentic leaders also continually assess and measure the value they bring. For example, implementing new assignments that leverage everyone's strengths can lead to increased efficiency, productivity, and customer satisfaction. This, in turn, can result in more revenue for the company and more referrals. Investing in people can have a lot of downstream impacts, both good and bad. However, if you tap into the good, there are no limits. Knowing the value you bring to the table is crucial for authentic leadership.

Authentic leadership means using your strengths courageously. It's not about fitting in; it's about finding a place that matches your values and boosts your strengths. An authentic leader knows what they can do and makes a space where these skills flourish, helping themselves and their teams.

Authentic leaders stand out for their consistent dedication to honesty, openness, and reliability. They understand their strengths and leverage them to foster an environment where authenticity is not only welcomed but celebrated. Authentic leadership is not merely a characteristic; it's a transformative force.

The influence of an authentic leader is real. It shows in the productivity of a team that leverages each member's talents and in the happiness of customers who benefit from the outcomes of a balanced team. An authentic leader restructures tasks to maximize team potential, leading to increased productivity and revenue. This is not just effective management; it's a testament to leadership that recognizes the significant impacts of investing in people.

A leader who is authentic has self-awareness. They know their strengths and weaknesses, values, and beliefs well. They reflect on themselves and how their decisions align with their core principles. A leader who is self-aware deals with the challenges of leadership with a clarity that builds trust and loyalty.

Authentic leaders are transparent. They don't just share what they decide, but also why they decide it. It's about acknowledging mistakes and transforming them into learning opportunities. This openness signals a commitment to honesty that cultivates a culture of trust and respect.

Building relationships is a skill that authentic leaders excel at. It's the emotional intelligence that enables them to connect with their team on a deeper level. Empathy and understanding are key to fostering unity and collaboration. When leaders prioritize these connections, they build teams that are not only effective but also resilient.

Authentic leadership is more than a concept; it's a way of acting that works in different contexts and scenarios. Here are some instances of how I used the ideas of authentic leadership in my work and life.

- **Self-awareness:** I regularly assessed my strengths and weaknesses as a leader and sought feedback from others to improve myself. I also reflected on my values and beliefs and how they influenced my actions and decisions. I recognized that being self-aware meant being humble and willing to learn from my mistakes and successes.

- **Transparency:** I communicated openly and honestly with my team, sharing my vision, goals, and expectations. I also explained the reasons behind my decisions and invited input and feedback from others. I admitted when I was wrong and apologized sincerely. I valued honesty and integrity above all else and expected the same from my team.

- **Building relationships:** I cared about my team as individuals, not just as employees. I listened to their concerns, needs, and aspirations and supported them in achieving their goals. I also celebrated their achievements and recognized their contributions. I showed empathy and understanding when they faced challenges and difficulties. I fostered a collaborative and supportive culture where everyone felt valued and respected.

These practices helped me become a more effective and authentic leader. They also enabled me to create a positive and productive work environment where my team thrived and delivered excellent results. I hope that by sharing my stories, you will be inspired to apply these practices in your own leadership journey.

As we wrap up our chapter on *Applying Authenticity*, let's revisit the key takeaways:

- Authentic leadership is characterized by self-honesty, ethical integrity, and the cultivation of genuine relationships with team members.
- A key aspect of authentic leadership is focusing on one's strengths and creating environments where these attributes can flourish.
- Transparency and self-awareness are crucial elements for authentic leaders, guiding their decisions and actions.

- Building relationships and connecting with the team on a deeper level is a skill that authentic leaders excel at.

Consider these reflection questions to deepen your understanding:

- How can you leverage your strengths to foster an environment that values authenticity?
- In what ways can you assess and measure the value you bring to your team?
- How can you increase transparency in your decision-making processes?

CHAPTER 9: CONTINUOUS LEARNING

The pursuit of authenticity is a perpetual classroom where the lessons are lived, and the living is learned.

Personal development is a lifelong journey and for leaders, it's a critical part of their professional growth. Effective leaders invest in their personal growth, equipping themselves with the skills required to lead their teams towards achieving their goals. Personal development strategies might include reading and learning about leadership theories, attending workshops or seminars, receiving coaching, and seeking feedback for improvement. These strategies can help leaders enhance their self-awareness, emotional intelligence, communication skills, decision-making abilities, and adaptability.

Reading and learning from different sources of knowledge is a simple and easy way to grow as a leader. This can include books, articles, podcasts, videos, or online courses that cover topics related to leadership, such as psychology, sociology, organizational behavior, business, or innovation. Reading and learning can expose leaders to different perspectives, frameworks, and best practices that can enrich their understanding of leadership and inspire them to try new approaches. Additionally, reading and learning can stimulate leaders' curiosity and creativity, which are essential for continuous learning and innovation.

Another way to boost leadership skills is to attend workshops or seminars that give hands-on and practical learning opportunities. Workshops or seminars can help leaders learn from experts, network with peers, and practice new skills in a supportive and constructive environment. Also, workshops or seminars can challenge leaders to stretch their limits, examine their assumptions, and receive useful feedback. By joining workshops or seminars, leaders can expand their leadership tools and techniques and customize them to their own contexts.

Coaching is a powerful form of personal development that can help leaders achieve their goals, overcome challenges, and unlock their potential. Coaching is a collaborative process between a coach and a coachee, where the coach asks open-ended questions, listens actively, and provides guidance and support. The coachee, on the other hand, sets the agenda, reflects on their situation, and takes action. Through coaching, leaders can gain clarity, confidence, and motivation to pursue their personal and professional aspirations. Coaching can also help leaders identify and address their blind spots, strengths, and areas for improvement.

Feedback is a key component for learning and growth, as it gives leaders feedback on how they perform, act, and influence. Feedback can come from various sources, such as supervisors, colleagues, subordinates, customers, or stakeholders. Feedback can be formal or informal, solicited or unsolicited, positive or negative, specific or general. Regardless of the source or type of feedback, leaders should welcome it as an opportunity to learn and grow. By seeking feedback for improvement, leaders can demonstrate their openness to change, appreciation of diverse opinions, and commitment to excellence.

Four personal development strategies that can help leaders are: reading and learning, workshops or seminars, coaching, and feedback. These strategies can enable leaders to improve their self-awareness, emotional intelligence, communication skills, decision-making abilities, and adaptability. They can also introduce leaders to different viewpoints, models, and best practices, as well as give them advice, assistance, and feedback for enhancement.

As we conclude this chapter, let's consider how these concepts of personal development play out in the day-to-day activities of leaders:

- **Example 1:** A consultant has been leading a team working on a complex project for a client. The consultant has been reading a book on leadership to better manage their team and deliver exceptional results. One concept they learned is the importance of regular feedback and open communication. The consultant decides to implement daily check-ins where each team member shares their progress and any blockers they're facing. This not only improves the team's communication but also allows the consultant to provide immediate feedback and assistance where needed.

- **Example 2:** A partner has been attending a leadership seminar. One of the key takeaways from the seminar was the importance of emotional intelligence in leadership. The partner realizes that understanding their team members' emotions and motivations can lead to a more harmonious and productive work environment. The partner starts to pay more attention to their team's dynamics, taking note of any conflicts or issues that arise. The partner also makes an effort to acknowledge and validate their team members' feelings during team meetings.

- **Example 3:** The CEO hired a leadership coach to help them navigate the challenges of running a new business. Through their coaching sessions, the CEO realizes that they have been micromanaging their team, which has been affecting their productivity and morale. With guidance from their coach, the CEO starts to delegate more tasks and trust their team's expertise. The CEO also sets up regular one-on-one meetings with each team member to discuss their goals and any challenges they're facing.

- **Example 4:** A team leader has been receiving feedback from his subordinates through an anonymous feedback system. One recurring piece of feedback is that the team leader needs to improve their communication skills. Taking this feedback to heart, the team Leader enrolls in a professional communication skills course. They also make an effort to be more clear and concise in their instructions and to actively listen when their team members are speaking.

These examples show how leaders can apply personal development strategies in their day-to-day activities to improve their leadership skills and create a more effective and harmonious work environment. Remember, personal development is a lifelong journey, and there's always room for improvement and growth.

As we wrap up our chapter on *Continuous Learning*, let's revisit the key takeaways:

- Personal development is a lifelong journey critical for leaders' growth.
- Reading and learning from diverse sources stimulates leaders' creativity and broadens their perspectives.
- Workshops and seminars provide leaders with practical experiences and opportunities to network.
- Coaching is a powerful tool that helps leaders unlock their potential and achieve their goals.
- Feedback is a key component for a leader's learning and growth.

Consider these reflection questions to deepen your understanding:

- What strategies are you employing for your personal development as a leader?
- Can you share a recent piece of learning that has significantly influenced your leadership style?
- Could you share a key learning experience from a recent workshop or seminar you attended?
- If you've had coaching, how has it benefited your leadership journey?

- Can you share an instance where feedback led to significant growth in your leadership journey?

CHAPTER 10: THE 30-DAY AUTHENTIC LEADERSHIP CHALLENGE

Challenge yourself to lead authentically, and watch as thirty days become a lifetime of impact.

In this challenge, you will complete one activity each day for 30 days. Each activity is designed to help you develop and practice the skills and habits of authentic leadership. You can choose to do them in any order but try to complete them all by the end of the month. You can also choose to share your experience and progress online using the hashtag **#AuthenticLeadership30**. This way, you can connect with other like-minded people who are taking the challenge and support each other along the way.

Here are the 30 activities for the challenge:

- **Day 1:** Write down your core values and why they matter to you as a leader.

- **Day 2:** Reflect on a situation where you acted in alignment with your values as a leader and how it made you and others feel.

- **Day 3:** Reflect on a situation where you acted against your values as a leader and how it made you and others feel.

- **Day 4:** Identify a goal that aligns with your values and purpose as a leader and write down the steps to achieve it.

- **Day 5:** Take one action toward your goal today and share your progress online.

- **Day 6:** Find a role model or mentor who embodies authentic leadership and reach out to them for advice or feedback on your leadership style.

- **Day 7:** Give honest and constructive feedback to someone you lead or work with and help them improve or grow.

- **Day 8:** Ask for honest and constructive feedback from someone you lead or work with and use it to improve or grow.

- **Day 9:** Write down three strengths and three areas of improvement as a leader.

- **Day 10:** Choose one area of improvement and commit to working on it for the next 20 days.

- **Day 11:** Practice active listening with someone you lead or work with today. Pay attention to their words, tone, body language, and emotions.

- **Day 12:** Practice empathetic communication with someone you lead or work with who you disagree with or find challenging. Try to understand their perspective and feelings without judging or criticizing them.

- **Day 13:** Practice assertive communication with someone who has authority or influence over you or your work. Express your opinions, needs, and boundaries clearly and respectfully.

- **Day 14:** Share a personal story or experience that illustrates your values or purpose as a leader with someone you lead or work with.

- **Day 15:** Share a vulnerability or challenge that you are facing or have faced as a leader with someone you lead or work with.

- **Day 16:** Recognize and appreciate someone who has helped or supported you in your leadership journey.

- **Day 17:** Apologize and take responsibility for a mistake or failure that you have made or contributed to as a leader.

- **Day 18:** Forgive and let go of a grudge or resentment that you have been holding onto as a leader.

- **Day 19:** Celebrate and reward yourself and your team for a success or achievement that you have accomplished or contributed to as a leader.

- **Day 20:** Learn something new that is relevant to your values, purpose, or goals as a leader. It can be a skill, a concept, a fact, or a perspective.

- **Day 21:** Teach someone else something that you have learned or know well and that is relevant to their values, purpose, or goals as a leader.

- **Day 22:** Seek out a different or diverse perspective on an issue or topic that you are interested in or passionate about as a leader.

- **Day 23:** Challenge yourself to step out of your comfort zone and do something that scares or intimidates you as a leader.

- **Day 24:** Delegate a task or responsibility that you can trust someone else to do well and that will help them grow or learn as a leader.

- **Day 25:** Collaborate with someone who has a different skill set or background than you on a project or problem that you both care about as leaders.

- **Day 26:** Support and empower someone who has less power or privilege than you in a situation where they need or want it as a leader.

- **Day 27:** Advocate and speak up for a cause or issue that aligns with your values and purpose as a leader and that affects you or others negatively.

- **Day 28:** Inspire and motivate someone who is struggling or feeling discouraged to keep going or try again as a leader.

- **Day 29:** Lead by example and demonstrate the behaviors and attitudes that you want to see in others as a leader.

- **Day 30:** Reflect on your journey and share your key learnings, insights, and outcomes online as a leader.

Congratulations! You have completed the 30-day authentic leadership challenge. I hope you liked this challenge and found it useful and rewarding. I also hope you will keep using and improving what you have learned and experienced in this challenge in your daily life. Authenticity is not a goal, but a practice. It's something you can develop and enhance every day, by being aware of your thoughts, feelings, and actions, by matching them with your values and purpose, and by expressing them with courage and compassion.

Thank you for taking this challenge and for being part of the **#AuthenticLeadership30** community. I wish you all the best in your future endeavors and I look forward to hearing from you soon.

CONCLUSION

In the end, authentic leadership is measured not by the echoes of one's words but by the footprints of one's actions.

You have reached the end of this book, and I hope you have enjoyed it as much as I have enjoyed writing it for you.

By completing this book and the challenge, you have taken a significant step toward becoming a more authentic leader in your personal and professional life. You have gained a deeper understanding of yourself, your values, your purpose, and your impact. You have also acquired the abilities and practices that will enable you to act, communicate, inspire, and collaborate as a leader based on your genuine self. You have also experienced the benefits of being more authentic, such as increased trust, engagement, performance, collaboration, innovation, and well-being.

However, your journey does not end here. Authenticity is not a static state, but a dynamic process. It's something you can always refine and improve, by staying true to yourself and adapting to your environment. It's also something you can always share and spread, by inspiring and empowering others to be more authentic as well. Authenticity is not only a personal quality, but a collective force. It's what makes us human, and what makes us leaders.

Therefore, I invite you to keep practicing and applying what you have learned and experienced in this book and the challenge. Keep being aware of your thoughts, feelings, and actions, and match them with your values and purpose. Keep expressing yourself with courage and compassion, and listen to others with openness and empathy. Keep seeking feedback and learning from your mistakes, and give feedback and recognition to others. Keep holding yourself and others accountable, and forgive yourself and others when needed. Keep celebrating your achievements and rewarding yourself and others, and keep facing new challenges and opportunities for growth.

Above all, keep being yourself, and keep being a leader. That's the best gift you can give to yourself, to others, and to the world.

ACKNOWLEDGEMENTS

I would like to express my gratitude to all the people who supported me in writing this book and helped me share my message of authenticity with the world. I am indebted to my family, friends, and mentors, who encouraged me, inspired me, and challenged me to grow and learn. And I am deeply thankful to you, my readers, for joining me on this journey and trusting me with your stories. You are the reason I wrote this book, and I hope it serves you well.

AUTHOR BIO

Hello! My name is Natasia Nolan-Hodge, and I'm a Human Capital Strategist with a wealth of experience that spans 26 years in the workforce and 18 years of honing my skills in Human Resources. My professional path has involved working with different HR sectors (e.g., Consulting, Corporate, and Federal), delivering customized HR services to both corporate businesses and federal agencies. My goal—and my passion—is helping people discover their inherent abilities and reach their objectives, as well as improving organizational performance.

Follow me on LinkedIn
https://www.linkedin.com/in/natasiahodge/

CONTINUE THE JOURNEY

Unleash the Leader Within Course

To continue on your authentic leadership journey, consider the Unleash the Leader Within course:

Tailored for aspiring leaders or those seeking to refine their leadership skills, this program guides you in building trust and leading with integrity, addressing fears of inadequacy and ensuring a lasting impact.

https://www.insp1ration.com/unleashtheleaderwithin

Unlock and Achieve Coaching Program

If you are seeking to uncover your hidden potential and develop customized strategies to get ahead, consider the Unlock and Achieve Coaching Program:

The Unlock and Achieve Coaching Program is specifically designed for those feeling stuck, uncertain, or underwhelmed by their professional journey. This program targets your unique challenges, offering customized strategies to guide you over hurdles and help you reach unprecedented professional heights. It's an intensive, focused approach to coaching that addresses common fears such as remaining static in your career, the anxiety of undefined professional paths, or the dread of not leveraging your full potential.

https://www.insp1ration.com/unlockandachievecoachingprogram

One-on-One Coaching

If you'd like coaching in a private setting, consider personal coaching.

https://www.insp1ration.com/coaching-learning

www.ingramcontent.com/pod-product-compliance
Lightning Source LLC
Chambersburg PA
CBHW07070524026
45472CB00023B/1483